T0194880

I'M UP

Soul Devotions for Seniors

BEVERLY BEEGHLY AVERS AND CONTRIBUTORS

WESTBOW
PRESS®
A DIVISION OF THOMAS NELSON
& ZONDERVAN

Copyright © 2022 Beverly Beeghly Avers and Contributors.

All rights reserved. No part of this book may be used or reproduced by
any means, graphic, electronic, or mechanical, including photocopying,
recording, taping or by any information storage retrieval system
without the written permission of the author except in the case of
brief quotations embodied in critical articles and reviews.

WestBow Press books may be ordered through booksellers or by contacting:

WestBow Press
A Division of Thomas Nelson & Zondervan
1663 Liberty Drive
Bloomington, IN 47403
www.westbowpress.com
844-714-3454

Because of the dynamic nature of the Internet, any web addresses or
links contained in this book may have changed since publication and
may no longer be valid. The views expressed in this work are solely those
of the author and do not necessarily reflect the views of the publisher,
and the publisher hereby disclaims any responsibility for them.

Any people depicted in stock imagery provided by Getty Images are
models, and such images are being used for illustrative purposes only.
Certain stock imagery © Getty Images.

ISBN: 978-1-6642-5400-8 (sc)
ISBN: 978-1-6642-5401-5 (hc)
ISBN: 978-1-6642-5399-5 (e)

Library of Congress Control Number: 2021925646

Print information available on the last page.

WestBow Press rev. date: 01/22/2022

"New Revised Standard Version Bible, copyright 1989, Division of Christian Education of the National Council of the Churches

Scripture taken from The Message. Copyright © 1993, 1994, 1995, 1996, 2000, 2001, 2002. Used by permission of NavPress Publishing Group.

Scripture taken from the Amplified Bible, Copyright © 1954, 1958, 1962, 1964, 1965, 1987 by The Lockman Foundation. Used with permission.

Revised Standard Version of the Bible, copyright 1952 [2nd edition, 1971] by the Division of Christian Education of the National Council of the Churches of Christ in the United States of America. Used by permission. All rights reserved.

Scripture quotations taken from The Holy Bible, New International Version® NIV® Copyright © 1973 1978 1984 2011 by Biblica, Inc. TM. Used by permission. All rights reserved worldwide.

Scriptures and additional materials quoted are from the Good News Bible © 1994 published by the Bible Societies/HarperCollins Publishers Ltd UK, Good News Bible© American Bible Society 1966, 1971, 1976, 1992. Used with permission.

CONTENTS

✵

ACKNOWLEDGMENTS

I would like to thank my daughter Diane Linton and friend Sylvia Bower for reading the manuscript and giving me suggestions for improvement. I thank Diane for all her help setting up my new computer. I give gratitude to Rebecca Chambers for creating the graphic design for the cover of the book. I am grateful to my daughter Kathy Moore, who wrote the devotion on what she learned caring for her father. It was my privilege and honor to receive the devotions written by my friends for this book: Rev. Sandra Huber; Barbara Davids; Rev. Dr. Crystal Walker and her father, Eddie Phelps; Rev. Beverly Schmidt; Rev. David Woodyard; Sue Sheets; Nancy Johnston; Sylvia Bower; and Rev. John Osborne.

I thank the staff from WestBow Press for their assistance in the publication of this book.

And most of all, I give God the glory with the direction of the Holy Spirit for the creation of *I'm Up.* Glory to God!

"O God, You are my God, I seek You, my soul thirsts for You. ----- Because Your steadfast love is better than life, my lips will praise You. So I will bless You as long as I live; I will lift up my hands and call on Your name. My soul is satisfied as with a rich feast, and my mouth praises You with joyful lips" (Psalm 63:1, 3–5).

INTRODUCTION

God is pursuing you, and God loves you, _____ (your name). God created you to love, enjoy, and be in communication with Godself. Come and sit a spell with your Abba, Daddy, Father. The devotionals in this book are for you to ponder, laugh at, meditate on, be inspired by, to face reality with, engage in, and enjoy our Lord on earth as it is in heaven. Come with me as we discuss our daily challenges. When it's time to go home, we will be lifted up to be with Jesus, unafraid and confident in God's eternal promises.

A. W. Tozer, author, tells us, "We pursue God because and only because God has first put an urge within us that spurs us to the pursuit. ... The impulse to pursue God originates with God, but the outworking of that impulse is our following hard after Him and all the time we are pursuing Him we are already In God's hand: 'Thy right hand upholdeth me.'"[1]

On a retreat I attended while at seminary, we were encouraged to walk around campus and be aware of the place that invited you to come and sit. A bench beckoned me, and I relented and reclined. We were to sit and enjoy the presence of our Lord. I found this moment to be helpful and special.

I want to encourage you to walk around your house, condo, apartment, patio, or garden and become aware of the area that is inviting you in, where the Lord is beckoning you to come each day. Then decide on a time—morning, noon, evening, or whenever—to meet daily with God. Make this your "appointment with God" time, and enjoy. Bring your Bible, pencil, and paper, go to your chosen place, and rest in the Lord's company.

This book is written for seniors but can also be used for family and friends as a conversational opener. Enjoy communicating your thoughts with each other. Try it now.

I have included hymns at the end of some chapters to recite or sing along with. Some of our seniors remember the hymns even when memory declines.

God bless you and thank you for engaging in this book. May our Lord Jesus help you get up and rejoice to serve our Lord.

Love, Beverly

Day 1

I'M UP

I can do all things through Him
who strengthens me.
Philippians 4:13

The alarm goes off, and the music comes on to tell me it is time to get up. I toss and turn. I just want to stay in bed for a little longer.

I know you experience this also. It takes all my energy to get up. I would rather just stay here and not face what is required of me physically, mentally, and emotionally. Now it is time to get up, so let's change our focus and picture Jesus surrounding us with His love and strength, lifting us up.

We lift our eyes to Jesus, for where else can we turn? Then the love of Jesus lifts us up. As the African American spiritual "Jesus Lifted Me"[2] states,

"I'm so glad Jesus lifted me.
I'm so glad Jesus lifted me."

"I'm up!" Thank You, Jesus.
Now help me, Jesus, to get dressed.

St. Paul tells us what to put on spiritually; we are to clothe ourselves in a new wardrobe.

"So, chosen by God for this new life of love, dress in the wardrobe God picked out for you: compassion, kindness, humility, quiet strength, discipline. Be even-tempered, content with second place, quick to forgive an offense. Forgive as quickly and completely as the Master forgave you. And regardless of what else you put on, wear love. It's your basic, all-purpose garment. Never be without it." (Colossians 3: 12-14) (The Message)

Prayer

Oh, Lord, I thank You for helping me to get up. Thank You for being beside me, around me, and even before me as You prepare the day. Oh, Lord, guide me, nudge me with the Holy Spirit, and direct me as I live one moment and one day at a time. It is a new day, so ignite my being toward a positive attitude as I put on Your garments, especially the garment of love shining forth Your love for all.

Read or sing the following African American spiritual hymn
"I'm so glad Jesus lifted me":

"I'm so glad Jesus lifted me.
I'm so glad Jesus lifted me,
I'm so glad Jesus lifted me.
Singin' Glory, Hallelujah, Jesus lifted me."

Day 2

BE STILL AND KNOW

*Be still, and know that I am God! I am
exalted among the nations, I am exalted
in the earth. The Lord of hosts is with
us; the God of Jacob is our refuge.*
Psalm 46:10–11

Imagine a beautiful garden with the sun shining brightly on the flower of your choice, capturing your attention. The waterfalls flow, creating a roaring yet calming sound. Just listen to the birds singing, giving you a message from your heavenly Father, God Almighty. There is a stillness all around that brings a peace that surpasses all understanding, and you know God is present with you. Now this is what God desired at the beginning of time— to meet with His created man and woman in His magnificent garden. A time to meet with one another and to enjoy one another's presence. Meditate on this scripture again and sit in peace.

Be still and know that I am God! -----

God is our refuge and strength, a very present help in trouble. Therefore we will not fear though the earth should change, though the mountain shake in the heart of the sea; though its waters roar and foam, though the mountains tremble with its tumult.------

God is in the midst of the city; it shall not be moved; God will help it when the morning dawns. The nations are in an uproar, the kingdoms totter; he utters his voice, the earth melts. The Lord of hosts is with us; the God of Jacob is our refuge.

(Psalm 46:10, 1–3, 5)

God is in the midst of all our concerns, difficulties, heartaches, and misunderstandings. Be still and rest. Allow God's peace to enfold you while you sit in silence. Breathe, be still, and when you are ready, talk with God as your friend and share what is in your heart.

Create your own prayer, or use this one:

Oh, Lord, it feels so good to be in Your presence. Give me faith to see that You are sovereign, that You have all things under control. Help me to trust You with all that is happening in our nation and the world. Come, Holy Spirit, and speak to me and help me to hear God's directives. Give me Your vision to see You all around me. Awaken my soul as I give You praise for all my many blessings. Then, may the peace of God, which surpasses all understanding, come and guard my heart and mind in Christ Jesus, my Lord. In Jesus's name I pray. Amen.

Sing or read the hymn
"In the Garden" by C. Austin Miles, 1913:

"I come to the garden alone
while the dew is still on the roses,
and the voice I hear falling on my ear,
the Son of God discloses.
And He walks with me,
and He talks with me,
and He tells me I am His own;
and the joy we share as we tarry there,
none other has ever known."

Day 3

CHILDLIKE

*And he said: "I tell you the truth, unless
you become like little children, you will
never enter the kingdom of heaven."
Matthew 18:3 (New International Version)*

Jesus said we must become like children to enter the kingdom
of God. Well, I qualify, for I now wear depends (like diapers),
take gummy supplements for calcium, use a walker or cane, and
need help from family with items I can't reach, forms I don't
understand, and cans and jars that are impossible for me to open.

Jesus tells us to accept and receive God's kingdom in the
same way a child accepts something. A young child trusts he or
she will be cared for, fed, clothed, and protected and is confident
that needs will be met. As we trust, we can rely on, lean on, and
be confident that God's promises are true.

As an early intervention specialist many years ago, I worked with babies and infants. I used a flashlight or toy to track, follow, and attend to the infant's eye movements. We as God's children do likewise—to attend to Jesus and to follow and trust the Spirit's leading. Children trust their parents or caregivers to provide for their needs.

Jesus calls us to do the same.

"Trust in the Lord with all your heart, and do not rely on your own insight. In all your ways, acknowledge him and he will make straight your paths. Do not be wise in your own eyes; fear the Lord, and turn away from evil. It will be a healing for your flesh and a refreshment for your body."(Proverbs 3:5-8)

"For the Lord is my Shepherd (to feed, guide and shield me); I shall not lack" (Psalm 23:1 Amplified).

I am now facing the decision to downsize my belongings and enter the Wesley Glen Retirement Community. I find it more difficult to do daily tasks, and I need assistance at times. I trust the Lord as God directs me. When I toured the apartment there, I looked out the window and saw this beautiful creek filled with all kinds of rocks.

Oh my, I thought, *what a God-wink, for I loved to creek-walk as a child*. This was the assurance that I was in the right place with the Lord's approval.

We trust more as we get older. Who do you trust? Family, a doctor, a caregiver, a physical therapist or occupational therapist?

Do you trust our Lord? "Even to your old age I am he, even when you turn gray I will carry you. I have made, and I will bear; I will carry and will save" (Isaiah 46:4).

God tells us we will be carried even as we grow older. Praise God. We can trust our Lord as God carries and directs us each day.

Let us pray: Oh, Lord, help me to trust You, to give myself to You as You lead me at this time in my life. Help me rely on You, lean on You, and listen to Your directives. I need help in so many areas, and I need Your assurance that all is well. Be with me as I keep focused on You and trust You as Your beloved child. In Jesus's name I pray. Amen.

Sing or speak the words to the hymn "Trust and Obey" by John H. Sammis, 1887:

"When we walk with the Lord in the light of His word,
What a glory He sheds on our way!
While we do His goodwill, He abides with us still,
and with all who will trust and obey.
Trust and obey, for there's no other way
To be happy in Jesus, but to trust and obey."

I'M UP, STANDING ON FAITH

For God so loved the world that he gave
His only Son, that whoever believes in him
should not perish but have eternal life.
John 3:16 (Revised Standard Version)

John 3:16 is a favorite scripture. I memorized it at vacation Bible school, camp, and so forth. God loved all creation, grieved the fall of man and woman, and sent God's Son Jesus to restore all creation.

In faith, we believe Jesus was crucified, died, rose again, and was resurrected! Praise the Lord. In John 3:16, Jesus speaks directly to you and me.

So come, invite Jesus into your heart if you have not done so, and Jesus will live with you now and forever. Jesus says, "But the Advocate, the Holy Spirit, whom the Father will send in my name, will teach you everything and remind you of all that I have said to you." (John 14:26).

I am writing this during Holy Week, when Jesus was nailed to the cross for you and me. Picture all our wrongdoings, wrong choices, poor decisions, and sins nailed on Christ's cross so you and I could be forgiven. All our sins—past, present, and future—are nailed on that cross. Psalm 103:12 tells us, "As far as the east is from the west, so far he removes our transgressions from us."

"If we confess our sins, he who is faithful and just will forgive us our sins and cleanse us from all unrighteousness" (1 John 1:9).

Let us name and confess these sins, wrong decisions, and misunderstandings: _____. Now release and let them go. As pastor of the United Methodist Church, I say: In the name of Jesus Christ, you are forgiven.

Whew! That's the good news: believe, surrender all to Jesus, and share this good news with others. Take a breath and thank and praise God our Father for making it possible to be forgiven and to live forever in the presence of our Lord.

Prayer: O Lord, we are humbled, we are so grateful for sending Your only Son to die for us so we can live forever with You. Help us walk faithfully as we stand on your promises of life eternal. In Jesus name we pray. Amen

Sing or say the words to the hymn "Standing on the Promises," written by Russell Kelso Carter in 1886:

"Standing on the promises of Christ, my King,
Through eternal ages let his praises ring;
Glory in the highest, I will shout and sing,
Standing on the promises of God.
Standing, standing,
Standing on the promises of God my Savior;
Standing, standing,
I'm standing on the promises of God."

Day 5

MASKS/WRINKLES/
FREEDOM

*Surely he has borne our infirmities. But He was
wounded for our transgression, crushed for our
iniquities; upon him was the punishment that
made us whole, and by his bruises we are healed.*
Isaiah 53:4–5

Masks: oh, Lord, my mask has changed so much, for all these
wrinkles and age spots have made my appearance unknown to
me. I feel so much younger at times and age-appropriate other
times. It is so funny how I have worn masks for so many wounds
of insecurity that could be hidden. You see, these wounds were
like daggers to my heart, mind, and emotions. Words hurt and
go deep within our being/our soul. They remain there until we
look at them and give them to our Lord for healing.

17

Jesus was sent to help the broken hearted and bring release (see Psalm 34:18). We have accepted Jesus as the one who saves us. Because of grace and mercy, we can give our wounds to our Lord Jesus, who has been there with us in all we have experienced. We don't have to be embarrassed because our Lord already knows everything about us. Now let Jesus have all your burdens, hurts, and wounds that have scarred you all these years.

What are some wounds you have experienced? Being betrayed, forgotten, misunderstood, verbally abused, angry, or _____?

What hurts have you imposed on others that need forgiveness?

In Hebrews 4:14, we read that we are to approach the throne of grace with boldness so we can receive mercy and grace when we need it. Because of what Jesus has done for us, we can bring all to Jesus, who will erase and forgive all.

In prayer, name and release these hurts/offenses to our Lord. And now these masks of deception are gone. Praise God. Christ Jesus has healed our insecurities, for we have used Christ's powerful cleanser and have been made free of blemishes and made right in God's sight. For our God is a God of compassion and steadfast love. God has cast all our hurts, wounds, and misunderstandings into the depths of the sea; they are gone! Gone! He will again have compassion upon us; He will tread our iniquities underfoot. You will cast all our sins into the depths of the sea (see Micah 7:19).

Now accept that they are gone, never to be brought up again. We have experienced freedom and are free indeed. Praise the Lord!

Prayer: O Lord, I am humbled. You have removed my scars, deep hurts, and lingering negative thoughts. O Lord, thank You for forgiving me. Help me accept Your forgiveness and let go of these obstacles, hindrances, and disobedience that I have treasured falsely for so long. Help me release them to You and know they are at the bottom of the sea, never to be brought up again (see Micah 4). Help me to feel the relief of letting them be, as you have cleared my slate and freed me to be whole again. Forgive me for burying them and not facing them head on, but thank You for giving me the strength this day to confront them and let them go. Now, heavenly Father, help me focus on You, giving You the praise for all You have done for me. Help me "get up" and when I'm up to stay positive as I turn my eyes on You, Lord Jesus. In grateful praise in Jesus's name, I pray, amen.

Read or sing "What a Friend We Have
in Jesus" by Joseph M. Scriven, 1855:

"What a friend we have in Jesus,
All our sins and griefs to bear!
What a privilege to carry everything to God in prayer!
O what peace we often forfeit,
O what needless pain we bear.
All because we do not carry everything to God in prayer."

Day 6

GRACE, GRACE

*For by grace you have been saved
through faith, and this is not your
own doing; it is the gift of God.
Ephesians 2:8*

As a child on Christmas Eve, I would get so excited in anticipation of the gifts I would find under the tree. My siblings and I would wake up early in the morning and get mom and dad up so we could open our gifts. These gifts were special but they didn't last long. God's gift of grace lasts forever.

Grace is undisputed, unconditional, unmerited, non-judgmental love. It is an over-flowing, over-powering love that leaves us humbled before our Lord. In grateful praise, we fall humbly on our knees, not literally, as we would never get back up. Christ's death on the cross was very costly for Him as He gave His life for us with no debt for us.

God has given us God's special gift of grace. For our Lord lifts us up from our sorrow, despair, confusion, and anxiety giving us God's gift of grace each day, each moment.

In times of trial, GRACE is our own Humpty Dumpty, our brokenness that Jesus has put back together again through His forgiveness, mercy and love. Praise God!

God gave His Son, part of himself, so we could be part of Godself. God holds us in the palm of God's hand and calls us His "Beloved". We don't deserve any of this but that's what we call Grace, amazing grace.

Grace, grace, God's grace, I am overwhelmed with thankfulness for God's grace. God's grace, freely given to me by God, undeserved, yet lavished upon me.

I have seen God's grace, mercy and love ever present in my life, forgiving me, changing my thoughts, perceptions and filling me with God's Holy Spirit. I have experienced the death of my daughter, denial, misunderstandings in relationships, and divorce. But through it all God has shown me his amazing grace.

Sit back and ponder this free daily gift of grace given just for you. What does grace mean for you? How have you seen God's grace work in your life?

Now thank your heavenly Father for God's grace. And remember you are a masterpiece because you are a piece of the master.

Sing or say the words to the hymn:
"Grace Greater than our Sin" by Julia H. Johnston, 1911:

"Marvelous grace of our loving Lord, grace that exceeds our
sin and our guilt! Yonder on Calvary's mount our-poured,
there where the blood of the Lambs was split. Grace, grace,
God's grace, grace that will pardon and cleanse within; grace,
grace, God's grace, grace that is greater than all our sin!"

Day 7

I JUST DROPPED IT

*But strive first for the kingdom of God
and his righteousness, and all these
things will be given to you as well.*
Matthew 6:33

I just dropped it. I must pick it up. Whoop-de-doo, you might say. Well, it is a big deal now. I lean over carefully, grab the item, bring it back up, and not fall. It demands balance as I steady myself and regain stability. I cry out to the Lord to be with my muscles, my nerves as I require them to function. I know some of you experience this too.

I'm up, and thank you Lord for helping me get back up. I have discovered that I am more dependent on the Lord's help each day, as I believe you need help also. As we seek and ask for God's help physically, mentally, emotionally, and spiritually, we discover God is right there. Just as the Israelites had to collect manna every day for survival and not collect too much or save it for next the day. We too must come each day for the Lord to fill our soul.

As Paul tells us: "For whenever I am weak, then I am strong.'" (2 Corinthians 12:10). I am strong because God is with me: "I have chosen you and not cast you off; do not fear, for I am with you, do not be afraid, for I am your God; I will strengthen you, I will help you, I will uphold you with my victorious right hand" (Isaiah 41:9b–10).

Lord, be with our muscles and nerves as we rely on them to function. Help us keep focused as we bend and move and trust that we will come back up.

Sarah Young says in her book *Jesus Calling*: "I am training you in steadiness. Too many things interrupt your awareness of *me*. I know that you live in a world of sight and sound, but you must not be a slave to those stimuli. Awareness of me can continue in all circumstances, no matter what happens. This is the steadiness I desire for you. Don't let unexpected events throw you off course. Rather, respond calmly and confidently, remembering that I am with you. As soon as something grabs your attention, talk with me about it."

So refocus knowing God loves us and knows our weaknesses. It requires discipline as we walk with our Lord each day, taking one step of faith at a time, trusting God's guidance. The Lord promises to take our hand and guide us. So speak and seek God's presence and God will steady your steps, helping you keep your balance with the challenges life brings forth.

Prayer: Oh Lord, you are teaching us to be deliberate, to concentrate and stay in the moment. Now help us do the same with You. Help us keep our balance physically, mentally, and spiritually. Help us to focus on You and know that with You all things are possible as you give us the strength through Christ to be victorious. May we seek Your good pleasure throughout the day in all we do. In Jesus's name we pray, amen.

Sing or say the words to the hymn "Turn Your Eyes upon Jesus" by Helen Howarth Lemmel, 1922:

"Turn your eyes upon Jesus,
Look full in His wonderful face,
And the things of earth will grow strangely dim,
In the light of his glory and grace."

Day 8

GRANDMOTHER: WHERE'S MARY?

*In those days Mary set out and went with haste
to a Judean town in the hill country where she
entered the house of Zechariah and greeted
Elizabeth. When Elizabeth heard Mary's
greeting, the child leaped in the womb.*
—*Luke 1:39*

"Where's Mary? She is my granddaughter, and I fear for her life. I heard she went to see Elizabeth but travel there is so dangerous with thieves ready to attack and steal. I pray the Lord will protect her and keep her safe. She is so precious to me, so kind and considerate."

Time passes, and I hear Mary's steps. She enters, sits near me, and tells me that when she entered Elizabeth's house, her baby leaped for joy, acknowledging her child within.

Mary leans near me. "I need your love and prayers for this awesome call cradling the living son of God."

"Oh, Mary, you have my prayers each day. God bless you as you live out your call, I love you."

What an exciting event shared with her grandma.

As grandparents, we feel so helpless at times. We remember our youth and know the challenges, temptations, expectations, and surprises our loved ones will encounter. My three daughters went to Germany with their German class, and oh how I prayed for their safety. When my granddaughter Caitlin was in Mozambique with the Peace Corps for three years, I prayed for her safety. When my grandchildren Sean, Lindsay, and Kristin traveled overseas, my prayers were with them also. What a wonderful opportunity our children and grandchildren have to experience other cultures. But we must trust and give them to our Lord for His care and protection.

What can we do as grandparents when we have concerns for our grandchildren? We can pray, listen when they call, reach out, and text. We are to "Be still and know God is" (Psalm 46:10) as we let go and trust God for God's guidance. We are then to rest in God's promise: "for surely I know the plans I have for you, says the Lord, plans for your welfare and not for harm, to give you a future with hope" (Jeremiah 29:11–12). Isaiah 44:3b says: "I will pour my spirit upon your descendants and my blessing on your offspring."

Let us pray: Oh Lord, we lift our children and grandchildren to You for safe keeping. We cherish them as You created them to be so special to us. Keep them close, guide them, protect them, and help them listen to Your directions for their life. Be with their relationships as they seek Your wisdom and discernment. In Jesus's name we pray, amen.

Sing or say words to portions of the hymn
"Mary Did You Know?" by Mark Lowry, 1998:

"Mary, did you know that your baby boy
Will one day walk on water?
Mary, did you know that your baby boy
Will save our sons and daughters?
Did you know that your baby boy
Has come to make you new?
This child that you've delivered
Will soon deliver you."

Day 9

WHERE ARE THE EGGS?

*A cheerful heart is a good medicine, but
a downcast spirit dries up the bones.
Proverbs 17:22*

Where are the eggs? I'm searching the refrigerator, but they're not there. Wait—I took out an egg to make a sandwich just a few days go. Oh, this is so funny; we just have to laugh. Maybe the eggs are still in the trunk. Note: yes, my son-in-law found the eggs in the trunk. Ha.

You know, the older we get the more we forget. Sometimes it changes direction and I find the keys in the refrigerator. Or who knows the surprise places I left the items? the Spirit directs me and the item is found!

Oh, we just have to laugh once in a while. Laughter is such good medicine. Are you laughing, remembering where you found something misplaced? Please remember, share with friends, laugh a belly laugh, and you will feel better.

I'd like to share another rather embarrassing story. My husband and I moved to a large, remodeled farmhouse when he took the job as principal of a high school. We kept finding these strange-looking little brown balls around the house and didn't know their source. Well, we got several glass jars and put these droppings in the jars to see what would happen. Well, when I showed them to Mom, she and Dad just laughed and laughed, for they were mouse droppings. Oh, what did we expect the things to do in a jar? Ha.

Another story to share: One evening when I was staying with a friend, she yelled, "It's a bat, a bat!"

I ran in the room as she gave me a bat net. I saw the bat on the wall and swung the net. I missed it and I thought it went under the bed. I pulled the net under the bed and slowly pulled it out to see a brown sock. Oh we laughed and laughed.

I tried again and I caught the bat in the net, put a board over the opening, and ran down the steps, releasing it outside. Oh, how we have shared this story, laughing with our family and friends.

Now it is your turn to share your stories with your family, neighbors, and friends and just laugh. It is good for your soul!

Prayer: Dear heavenly Father, thank you for laughter that refreshes our souls. Help us to see Your little surprises, Godwinks, which bring smiles to our faces and chuckles to our being. We know it brings pleasure to You also when we can enjoy You and Your beautiful creation. In Jesus's name we pray, amen.

Sing or say words to the hymn, "Down In
My Heart" by George W. Cooke, 1977:

"I have the joy, joy, joy, joy down in my heart,
Down in my heart, down in my heart, down in my heart.
I have the joy, joy, joy, joy
Down in my heart to stay."

Day 10

PONDERING CHANGE
BY BARBARA DAVIDS

For I, the Lord, do not change.
Malachi 3:6

Many of us refer to our life as a journey. Along the way we experience up times and down dtimes. We see and have gone through many changes.

Daily on our journey we have seen rules change, families change, and communication methods change from rotary dial phones to cell phones. Clothing styles have changed as well. Have you seen grandma in blue jeans and sneakers?

The seasons change as well as methods of travel. Remember the horse and buggy? What about a horse and a single plow blade? Today it's giant tractors and massive cultivators.

A grandson marries and becomes a father. Suddenly there is a new reality—my daughter is a grandma! Now change has shown me I am old.

One could go on and enumerate the many changes we have encountered and lived through. Photos show our appearance has changed. We make plans, but again and again some last-minute issue comes up and requires us to change our plans.

As an over-eighty elder, change seems to come more often and quickly. Or is it me slowing down?

Perhaps our focus needs to change! Consider the word *constant*. Is there anything constant in your life, anything *unchangeable*?

Let us ponder the scriptures.

"For I the Lord, do not change" (Malachi 3:6).

"Be still and know that I am God" (Psalm 46:10).

"God is our refuge and strength, a very present help in trouble" (Psalm 46:1).

"Come to me, all you all you that are weary and are carrying heavy burdens, and I will give you rest" (Matthew 11:28).

Prayer: Dear Lord, we need thee every hour, keep us in your everlasting arms, we know you knock and we ask you to please come in. Thank you for your constant presence and guidance, we trust in you the one who holds the world and all things in your hands. Amen

Sing or read from the hymn:
"He Lives" by Alfred H. Ackley, 1933:

I Serve a Risen Savior, He's in the World Today":
"I know that He is living, whatever foes may say,
I see His hand of mercy, I hear His voice of cheer,
And just the time I need Him, He's always near.
He lives, He lives, Christ Jesus lives today!
He walks with me and talks with me along life's narrow way.
He lives, He lives, salvation to impart!
You ask me how I know He lives? He lives within my heart."

Day 11

BE STRONG AND COURAGEOUS BY REV. SANDRA HUBER

*Be strong and courageous; do not be
frightened or dismayed, for the Lord
is with you wherever you go.*
Joshua 1:9

I shared this verse recently in notes written to graduating high
school seniors. I thought about the new paths they were embarking
upon and how steps into an unknown future can be intimidating
and, sometimes, frightening. I hoped to convey an assurance of
God's presence with them as they travelled into new experiences.
As I thought about it more, I realized that this verse expresses an
important assurance for all of us as we journey through life from
youth to old age.

I am a planner. When possible, I like to anticipate the future and work toward it. Because of that, we recently remodeled our bathroom. We wanted to make it more accessible—just in case we need it. Our plan is to "age in place." I know that may not be possible.

I know there is no set path to aging and death. I have travelled with dear family members. We moved my in-laws from their home into assisted living and then into nursing care. My parents moved from their home into a life-plan community with all the stages of care but remained in independent living. My mother-in-law lived into her late eighties, my father-in-law into his early nineties, my dad into his mid-nineties, and my mother into her early hundreds. Each had a different journey. Only one seemed to go according to plan, and that was my father-in-law, who planted his last tomatoes and said he didn't want to see his next birthday. He didn't.

My dad hoped to live to one hundred, but in his early nineties said he didn't think he'd make it. He didn't. My mother-in-law planned to keep her mind active and clear with reading and crossword puzzles; strokes made that impossible. My mother had no aspirations to live long, but she did. And in living long she showed me how to embrace aging with grit and grace. She cared for my dad as dementia claimed his mind. She recovered from a broken hip in her late nineties. She cared for herself through healthy eating, regular exercise, commitment to learning, acceptance of change, relationships with friends and family, and regular worship attendance. She never failed to care and pray for others—those she knew and loved, as well as concerns of the world.

Each of our parents faced aging unafraid, with strength and courage. I am thankful for their examples, and I am confident they each knew the Lord was with them on the journey. I pray that I too will face aging with strength, courage, and the assurance that no matter what happens or where I am, God is with me.

How are you planning? What uncertainties do you feel? Where do you need strength, courage, and assurance of God's presence? How are you being an example to others?

Prayer: Omnipresent God, we are easily discouraged. Unexpected challenges and changes in plans upset and sometimes frighten us. We frequently yearn for what was instead of embracing Your presence in what is. Grant us wisdom, grant us courage for the living of each day knowing that You are with us in all times and all places. Amen.

Sing or say words to the hymn "God of Grace and
God of Glory" by Harry Emerson Fosdick, 1930:

"God of grace and God of glory, on thy people pour thy power;
Crown thine ancient church's story; bring her bud to
glorious flower. Grant us wisdom, grant us courage, for
the living of these days, for the living of these days."

Day 12

PRESSING ON, PURSUING, PERSEVERANCE— THREE PS

*I press on to make it my own, because Christ
Jesus has made me His own. Beloved, I do
not consider that I have made it my own; but
this one thing I do: forgetting what lies behind
and straining forward to what lies ahead.*
Philippians 3:12–13

I have a paralyzed shoulder from a birth injury, but I had a great left-handed hook shot as a basketball player when I was in high school. My disability did not hold me back. I majored in physical education at Bowling Green State University. Now my good right arm is tired from overwork. I have trouble reaching items from the cupboard, dressing each morning, and lifting items. I press on. And you can too!

Pressing On: Let us keep pressing on with determination to keep looking forward toward our goal of keeping Christ Jesus first in our lives. Let us not look back, for God has forgiven us for our wrongdoings. God will have compassion on us and will cast all our sins into the depths of the sea (see Micah 7:19).

What is your challenge today? How will you keep pressing on? Set a goal.

Pursuing: Let us keep pursuing God, for God is pursuing us. Our souls are restless until they find fellowship with God. I see a reciprocal relationship with God. God pursues me with an encompassing and overflowing love. I respond humbly in grateful thankfulness to God. Picture God's love overflowing you and your love overflowing back to God in thankfulness. Pause, reflect, and give thanks

Perseverance: Let us keep persevering as we keep holding on to our rock, Jesus. "Brothers and sisters, do not be weary in doing what is right" (2 Thessalonians 3:13).

Perseverance is defined in The American Heritage Dictionary, New College Edition, as "The holding to a course of action, belief, or purpose without giving way, steadfastness".

I will persevere by (state your course of action):

_____

_____

Let us keep up the good work and not look back but *press on.* Let us continue to be in *pursuit* of our God as we meet with our Lord each day. Let us faithfully *persevere,* knowing our Lord is with us, giving us strength. For if we don't, all will go to *pot.* Ha. Did I hear a chuckle?

Prayer: Lord Jesus, I send an SOS! I need Your help not to give up, to stick with it, especially on difficult days. Help me press on as I pursue You faithfully with all my concerns, small or big. Help me persevere living as your faithful servant, bringing hope and love to all those you place on my path. Help me praise You for all my blessings during my daily challenges. Thank You, Holy Spirit, for guiding and directing me each day, making all things possible through Jesus Christ our Lord. In Jesus's name I pray. Amen.

Day 13

JESUS, JESUS, JESUS

*I will do whatever you ask in my name, so that
the Father may be glorified in the Son. If in my
name you ask me for anything, I will do it.*
John 14:13–14

When you call on the name of Jesus, there is just something
special about the name of Jesus. When serving as Pastor Bev, I
was humbled to have individuals share with me their intimate
secrets of sexual abuse, relationship dysfunctions, family
misunderstandings, and other circumstances, for the first time.
They came to me feeling sad, broken, and in need of help. We
prayed as I lifted the name of Jesus. I witnessed their countenance
change. They left refreshed, forgiven, and with a new attitude of
hope. All this done in the name of Jesus Christ, our Lord.

After I retired, I served as a volunteer on Kairos teams
(Christian women and men trained to lead retreats in prisons).

We went to the Marysville Ohio Reformatory Prison for women. Our team led a weekend retreat that brought the love of Jesus to these women. The ladies, our guests, came to the retreat broken, in despair, in need of forgiveness and hope. Forty inmates experienced the very Love of Christ Jesus as they called on the name of Jesus and told us of their transforming experiences. Jesus had entered their lives, giving them forgiveness, grace, mercy, and *love*.

In her devotional "Jesus Lives," Sarah Young writes: "Invite me (Jesus) into your thoughts by whispering my name; suddenly your day brightens and feels more user- friendly. When you speak my name in loving trust, you sense my Presence and feel yourself drawing close to me. As you look to me, *my face shines upon you* in radiant approval, brightening your day and helping you feel secure."

So I encourage you to say the name of Jesus often. When you don't have the words when you pray, just say: "Jesus." When you are scared, just say as you pray: "Jesus." When you are sad or lonely, just say: "Jesus." When you are in surgery, waiting, say: "Jesus." When you just found out your relative, friend, or pet passed away and you are upset, say: "Jesus, help me, Jesus."

Prayer: Jesus, come, Lord Jesus, come, be near me this day. Fill my day with your love. Help me to say your name often, bringing me stillness, peace, assurance, love, and the ability to carry on. Help me to reach out to others showing your love to them. In Jesus's name I pray. Amen.

Read or sing the hymn
"His Name Is Wonderful" by Audrey Mieir, 1959:

"His name is wonderful,
His name is wonderful,
His name is wonderful, Jesus, my Lord.
He is the mighty King,
Master of everything,
His name is wonderful, Jesus my Lord."

"And the Lord bless you, and watch, guard, and keep you; the Lord make His face to shine upon and enlighten you and be gracious (kind, merciful, and giving favor) to you. The Lord lift up His (approving) countenance upon you and give you peace (tranquility of heart and life continually)" (Numbers 6:24–26 Amplified Bible).

Day 14

INTERTWINED
WITH JESUS

I am the Vine, you are the branches. Whoever
lives in Me and I in him bears much (abundant)
fruit. However, apart from Me—cut off from
vital union with Me—you can do nothing.
John 15:5 (Amplified)

We are intertwined with Jesus—connected, complete, one. The
Holy Spirit has made it possible for us to love Jesus. We do not
have to be in this world alone; we have Jesus within.

Sarah Young tells us in her book *Jesus Calling*: "I am Christ in
you, the hope of Glory. The One who walks beside you, holding
you by your hand, is the same One who lives within you. This
is a deep, unfathomable mystery. You and I are *intertwined* in an
intimacy involving every fiber of your being. The Light of my
Presence shines within you, as well as upon you. I am in you,

and you are in me; therefore nothing in heaven or on earth can separate you from me!"

Why is it so difficult for us to believe that Jesus lives within us? We are so stiff-necked, wanting our own way, wanting the control button to be at our fingertips.

Young goes on to say: "As you sit quietly in my Presence, your awareness of my life within you is heightened. This produces the *Joy of the Lord,* which is your strength. I, the God of hope, fill you with all Joy and Peace as you trust in me, so that you may bubble over with hope by the power of the Holy Spirit."

In my book *Intertwined: Beverly & Barbara in the Womb*, I state that "as a fetus I became aware and conscious that something else was beside me in the womb. As I became more aware, Barbara and I poked at each other; we laughed, had our own language as Barbara and I were intertwined." I ask you to imagine Jesus close to you, connected, living within you, seeking your attention and love. Pause. Allow the presence of Jesus to come upon you. Be still and know God is in your midst.

I suggest in the book that we use the breath prayer to help stay connected with Jesus. The way to use the breath prayer: *inhale* and say: "Jesus, have mercy on me," and *exhale* and say: "I am intertwined with Jesus." Breathe and repeat. Then throughout the day you can use your breath prayer and remember to whom you belong. For you are intertwined with Jesus; allow the Holy Spirit to direct you, guide you, and love you each day and moment.

Prayer: Oh Lord, I am intertwined with You, Jesus. Help me stay connected with You as I live this day. Holy Spirit, remind me I am not alone and nothing can separate me from You.

Now breathe in and say: "Jesus, have mercy on me." Exhale and say: "I am intertwined with Jesus." Repeat. In Jesus's name, I pray.

Sit quietly for a while and relax and breathe.

Sing or say the words:
"Oh How I Love Jesus" by Frederick Whitfield, 1855:

"There is a name I love to hear; I love to sing its worth.
It sounds like music in my ear, the sweetest name on earth.
O how I love Jesus, O how I love Jesus,
O how I love Jesus,
Because he first loved me!"

OUR INHERITANCE

*For you did not receive a spirit of slavery to fall
back into fear, but you have received a spirit of
adoption. When we cry, "Abba! Father!" it is
that very Spirit bearing witness with our spirit
that we are children of God, and if children,
then heirs, heirs of God and joint heirs with
Christ—if, in fact, we suffer with him so
that we may also be glorified with him.*
Romans 8:15–17

In the Message (Bible translation) states it as: "This resurrection
life you received from God is not a timid, grave-tending life. It's
adventurously expectant, greeting God with a childlike 'What's
next, Papa?' God's Spirit touches our spirits and confirms who we
really are. We know who he, is and we know who we are—Father

and children. And we know we are going to get what's coming to us—an unbelievable inheritance!"

My heart sings, my fingers tingle, and my soul rests when I read Romans 8. We belong! You and I have a heavenly Abba-Daddy, Papa, Father. We are God's beloved child, precious in God's sight. Have you always wanted to belong? Have you wanted to be part of something and just felt left out? Please know you are part of God's family, for God has adopted you and made you His own. As God's child, you and I inherit God's treasures. We will live forever with our Father, being more secure and of more worth than any of our IRAs or 401Ks.

We have completed our wills, and I hope you have completed yours. In our wills we designated who would be our beneficiaries. Now we are God's beneficiaries to receive all God's benefits, which last forever.

_____ (Your Name) is entitled to receive God's benefits on: Date: Forever.

Pause and thank our loving Father and Jesus for this grateful gift to you.

I encourage you to be part of a church family for support and to give support as we belong and inherit God's blessings.

Please read Psalm 103:1–5:

Bless the Lord, O my soul, and all that is within me, bless his holy name. Bless the Lord, O my soul, and do not forget all his benefits—who forgives all your iniquity, who heals all your diseases, who redeems your life from the pit, who crowns you with steadfast love and mercy, who satisfies you with good as long as you live so that your youth is renewed like the eagle's.

Prayer: Abba, Father, thank you for adopting us as your children. May we humbly praise you and honor you as our Abba, heavenly Father. We thank you for all the gifts that we have inherited through Christ; our salvation, forgiveness, grace, mercy, love and eternal life. We give You our Praise and thankfulness this day. In Jesus's name we pray. Amen.

Sing or read "Jesus Loves Me" by Anna B. Warner, 1860:

Jesus Loves Me This I know, for the Bible Tells Me So
Little ones to Him belong;
They are weak but He is strong.
Yes, Jesus loves me!
Yes, Jesus loves me!
Yes, Jesus loves me!
The Bible tells me so."

Day 16

CREATION CARE BY DR. REV. CRYSTAL WALKER WITH HER FATHER EDDIE PHELPS

In the beginning God created the
heavens and the earth.
Genesis 1:1

God saw all that he had made,
and it was very good.
Genesis 1:31 (NIV)

Eddie: I grew up in the 1940s. My family was charged to take care of the land and animals. We farmed, grew crops, tended animals, and took care of God's creations. In my eighty-plus years on earth, I have seen so many animals go into extinction. I have witnessed the change of the land from a rich, growing, and vibrant field to what some would have described my family as dirt poor. It is disheartening to see what has happened to God's land and animals and what is still happening today.

Crystal: Although the pandemic has caused many deaths and illnesses, it has also been an opportunity for God's land and creation to rest and heal. Carbons are not polluting the air as much. Animals are not being murdered because of too much development or toxins. And we as a nation that is busy, busy, busy are having to be still if just for a moment. Yes, the pandemic is causing economic woes, family stress, and mental concerns. But if we would think just for a second on what this pandemic has done to help us get closer to God, we would praise God anyhow.

Eddie: We are all part of God's creation, and we must treat God's land, God's creatures, and God's humanity with love and respect. Genocide of any of God's creation should not be tolerated.

Crystal: Let us pray together that we learn to love, respect, and cultivate all of God's creation so that all may be well in the land and heal.

Prayer: Genesis 1:1 says, "In the beginning, God created the heavens and the earth." Oh, God, You have created for Your glory and our enjoyment the heavens and the earth. For Your glory, Lord, we repent that we have not taken care of Your creation. For Your glory, God, we admit that our possessions and greed have caused the beauty of heaven and earth to diminish. For our enjoyment, Lord, we admit that we enjoy man made things instead of the beauty of heaven and earth, and for this enjoyment we have lost much of our forests and nature. Our possession and greed has caused global warming, unprecedented storms, wildfires, and so many actions against nature. We come to You today to seek forgiveness, to seek wisdom, and to ask You to replenish our land. It is in Jesus's name we pray. Amen.

I KNOW GOD CARES BY REV. BEVERLY SCHMIDT

The earth dries up and withers, the world
languishes and withers; the heavens languish
together with the earth. The earth lies polluted.
Isaiah 24:4–5

Our Bible study this year is on lament. We want to learn together how to pray our deepest worries and concerns to God while reassuring ourselves that God hears us and cares. There is no end to the laments we have now in the early part of the twenty-first century over God's creation. When we remember our childhood—the clear, running creeks; the always-fresh air; clean oceans full of fish, many varieties of wild animals and insects in the abundant woods and forests—we lament the change in our lifetime to a more polluted and dangerous environment. It is hard for me to imagine the people in Isaiah's time would have had the same lament we have.

Does our Creator God know about this change in today's world? we might ask. I need only to mention one pollution problem to illustrate the situation. It is said the plastic pollution in the oceans is enormous. The Great Pacific Garbage Patch is an area twice the size of Texas. Yet while I know this is true, I order meals from the dining room in our retirement home delivered in plastic containers. The containers assure us our food is at a delicious peak of taste and appearance. The containers cannot be recycled, so they are put into the trash. The culinary department and residents lament our inability to solve this problem that adds to pollution. Does God know we need help with this? I ask.

Many years ago we lived in upstate New York. We loved the natural beauty of the area. It was a wonderful place to raise our children. However, the winters were very cold. We had friends whose parents wintered in Florida. I longed to take a break from the weather to visit parents in Florida as my friends were able to do. I didn't pray about it. God didn't need to hear me complain about a relatively small matter. Nevertheless, it was a nice change to move to central Ohio where the weather is less extreme. However, people in Ohio practically go to Florida as rite of passage in the winter. My longing to wander along a sandy seashore looking for the prettiest shell of the day, and to stand in the water and be rocked by the waves, was as great as my desire had been in New York.

Finally, Glen and I were truly and well retired. We rented a condo in Florida for the month of January. The first night I slipped into bed and lay my head on the pillow. It had a lovely scent. I thought it was nice that our landlord would have scented the pillowcase. But it was in no other place, not even on Glen's pillow. And it didn't last long. Quickly I realized it was a gift from God, just for me. God knew just how much I had longed for this holiday. God was sharing the joy with me.

So my reasoning goes like this: If God shares my longing for something as minor as a holiday by the seashore, something I didn't even bother to pray for, surely God is hearing the vast cries of lament over the increasing pollution and death and danger of our earthly environment. It took the better part of a lifetime for me to get to Florida, so let us not be impatient to get the problems of pollution sorted out. God is working with and through all the lamenters, and even among the climate deniers, to get Creation back on track. God is, after all, the Creator. Let's keep asking what we can do to help, and then be obedient servants in the recreation of our earthly home.

Prayer: Dear Creator and Loving Lord of all, help me remember the small, sweet surprises that have come from You. Hear my lament and add it to the others You hear so it becomes a great cry for justice upon the earth. Open our ears that all may hear that small, sweet word from You that tells us how to help. Amen.

Day 18

DOWN BUT NOT FORSAKEN BY REV. DAVID WOODYARD

*[Elijah] went a day's journey into the wilderness
and came and sat down under a solitary
broom tree. He asked that he might die: "It is
enough; now, O Lord, take away my life.*
1 Kings 19:4

*At three o'clock Jesus cried out with a loud voice,
"Eloi, Eloi, lema sabachthani?" which means,
"My God, my God, why have you forsaken me?"*
Mark 15:34

It's January 8, 2021, after midnight. I'm lying in a hospital bed. My back is aching, my legs are in compression hose, I can't find my call button, and I'm wearing a heart monitor, which I think has me chained to the wall. I'm miserable. I'm sinking into depression and wondering how I can end all this. I'm alone. I'm abandoned. I feel like death is the answer!

The door opens and a shaft of light beams across the room. A nurse asks how I am. "I'm miserable and want to die!" As we continue to talk, she takes the compressors off my legs, she assures me that my heart monitor is not attached to the wall, she puts the call button into my hand, and she says she'll get me some pain medication. I feel better.

God didn't abandon Elijah or Jesus, and God didn't abandon me either. Actually, I was given an opportunity to gain a bit of empathy for persons caught in depression and show how important light is and how interacting with a helpful, caring person can be healing.

Overcoming real depression is not simple, but it can be helped when the dark, debilitating isolation it drags people into is exposed to God's light and to caring persons who have the experience and wisdom to provide real help.

Prayer: Loving God, for those experiencing depression, I pray that they may be guided to your light and to caring, experienced persons who can give them hope through care-filled listening and helpful actions. Amen.

Day 19

WHERE TWO OR THREE ARE GATHERED BY SUE SHEETS

The steadfast love of the Lord never ceases, his
mercies never come to an end; they are new
every morning; great is your faithfulness.
Lamentations 3:22–23;

My journey of faith began six years ago. I work on my faith daily doing devotions and prayers. Within the past year I have begun to learn about the Holy Spirit and daily look for the Spirit's guidance and prayers.

Very soon into this journey I realized that I didn't feel love, something that I had never been felt in my heart. The feeling of love was brought to me by a special young lady (Rev. Avers's daughter) through her singing. She now lives with God. I will one day thank her.

This journey of faith was aided particularly by two small group ministries; Upper Room devotions at our church, and Riverbend Bible Study Condo ministry. My small groups have answered questions with Scripture that I did not understand. They were supportive when I had cataract and cornea surgeries and when the one cornea surgery failed. These ladies took me to appointments, to church, sent cards, and brought food, as well as phoned with prayers and good wishes. Upper room sisters blessed me twice with laying of hands when I was most apprehensive about the surgeries.

This devotional book is for us seniors, so I say to those of you who are feeling down, cheer up by cheering up others, such as those who are homebound. You can phone, text, write notes, and pray for them. I do all of these. Keep in contact with people. They will love you for it.

I will be eighty-four later in the year and look forward to continuing these suggested activities for many more years. As one ages, it becomes necessary to depend on help from others with activities that become difficult to perform on our own. This help might be from friends, neighbors, or social service agencies. If you need help, ask for it to keep you safe. Pastors, active and retired, as well as church staff give so much encouragement and help to all. Reach out to them when you need their help, support, and prayers.

I also hope you can get involved in a small group (ladies, men, couples) Bible study/support ministry at your church or community. It is so helpful to study, share, and pray together. God promises to be present: "For where two or three are gathered in name, I am there among them" (Matthew 18:20).

Prayer: Loving God, thank You for those who show us who You are through their love, example, and cheer. Help us to learn from them and share Your love with the world. Amen.

Sing or read the words to the hymn "Great Is Thy
Faithfulness" by Thomas O. Chisholm, 1923:

"O God, my Father, there is no shadow of turning with thee;
Thou changest not; thy compassions they fail not.
As thou has been thou forever wilt be.
Great is thy faithfulness!
Great is thy Faithfulness!
Morning by morning new mercies I see;
All I have needed thy hand hath provided.
Great is thy faithfulness.
Lord, unto me!"

Day 20

WHAT IS YOUR TEMPERATURE?

*You desire truth in the inward being; therefore
teach me wisdom in my secret heart.*
Psalm 51:6

*Create in me a clean heart, O God, and put a
new and right spirit within me. Do not cast me
away from your presence, and do not take your
holy spirit from me. Restore to me the joy of your
salvation and sustain in me a willing spirit.*
Psalm 51 10–12

During the Covid-19 epidemic, our temperature was taken every
time we entered a facility. My question for you today is: How is
your emotional temperature? Are you sad, angry, grieving, happy,
anxious, or jumpy? If you take your temperature, is it hot and

elevated from misunderstanding, disappointment, body challenges, or grief? When you sense it is high, what can you do to lower it?

1. **God's Command**. We are to love the Lord our God with all our heart, mind, and soul (Matthew 22:37). Meet with your Lord each day.

2. **Be Aware**: recognize and identify how you feel.

3. **Mind**: stop and breathe, refocus, redirect your mind when it tells you falsehoods, such as you're not good enough, you can't do something well. Address the thought, evaluate it, and if it is telling you something you need to work on, do so. If the thought is wrong, tell it you are not going to continue bringing this thought into your mind.

4. **Energy Level Low**: Time to rest, you don't have to justify taking a nap, your body is telling you to rest. My daughter Diane takes a twenty-minute power nap and she is rejuvenated. I need an hour nap. It is important to listen to your body and obey as the body informs you of the need to rest.

5. **Emotions**: If depressed: Call your counselor if you have one, or get one. Talk with your pastor or Stephen Minister. If you are very depressed and thinking suicide and need help now, do not wait! Call 1-800-273-8233 or www.suicidepreventionlifeline.org.

6. **Feeling Good**: observe, thank God, rest in God's peace and record/remember this temperature for future discernment.

7. **Get Up**: Praise God you're Up. Keep thanking God. Do what God tells you to do as you listen to God's directives as God's beloved child.

8. **Exercise**: Body: Do you not know that your body is a temple of the Holy Spirit within you, which you have from God, and that you are not your own? For you were bought with a price; therefore glorify God in your body. (I Corinthians 6:19-20). We are to take care of our body, it is not our own. Keep it fit for God's use, physically and in all areas.

9. **Joy Comes In The Morning**. If you are experiencing a difficult day, please remember tomorrow will come, just as the sun rises each morning bringing hope, promises and newness. In Psalm 30:5, ll-12) reads: "Weeping may linger for the night, but joy comes with the morning. You have turned my mourning into dancing; you have taken off my sackcloth and clothed me with joy, so that my soul may praise you and not be silent. O Lord my God, I will give thanks to you forever."

So wait, be patient, because tomorrow is a new day. You are God's beloved.

Prayer: Oh Lord, help me first to listen to you as I come to meet with You. Help me to listen to my body when it tells me to stop or slow down. Then give me the strength to get up and move, even when it would be easier to remain seated. Transform and renew my mind so I can know your will. Create in me a clean heart and right spirit within me. Keep my focus on you and divert my thinking when it becomes negative. Holy Spirit nurture my soul for you are my helper, comforter, strengthener as you help me know and love Jesus my Savior. My inner most being thirsts for You. Restore in me the joy of my salvation as you are so present within me. In Jesus's name I pray. Amen

Sing or read the hymn by Chris H. Scott, 1895:

"Open My Eyes That I May See":

Glimpses of truth thou hast for me,
Place in my hands the wonderful key
That shall unclasp and set me free.
Silently now I wait for thee, ready,
My God, thy will to see.
Open my eyes; illumine me, Spirit divine."

GRIEF BY SYLVIA BOWER AND BEVERLY AVERS

The Jews who were with her in the house,
consoling her, they saw Mary get up quickly and
go out. They followed her because they thought
that she was going to the tomb to weep there.
John 11:31

Hello, may I come and sit with you in your special place today? I know you are hurting and I grieve with you. There are no words, so my spirit, with the Lord Jesus, comes and sits with you now.

Shakespeare said in *Much Ado about Nothing*, "Everyone can master a grief but he that has it."

Grief is such a personal experience. There is no right or wrong, but each of us must go through the stages. Sometimes we bury our grief deep inside and do not acknowledge it for a long time. Our Lord knew how to grieve when he wept when Lazarus died.

It is emotionally and physically healthy to acknowledge what you perceive as a severe loss: to grieve, to cry, to become angry, and to not understand why. We might deny that a loved one is really gone. We become angry and feel like there is unfinished business, and we take those feelings out on others. We might try to bargain with God and say, "Why me? Why now?" Many will be depressed and feel worthless, and others may repress their grief feelings to the point of needing professional help.

When we grieve, sometimes we become immobilized to the point that our souls moan. Jesus knows what you need, and He wants you to ask Him for His help. The most important step in this process is acceptance. As you realize that God is in control and you really need His help, you can now move on with life.

"Do not worry about anything, but in everything by prayer and supplication with thanksgiving let your requests be known to God. And, the peace of God, which surpasses all understanding, will guard your hearts and your minds in Christ Jesus" (Philippians 4:6–7).

Breathe, and "Be still and know I am God." (Psalm 46: 10) Mary and Martha's friends came and stayed with them as they mourned the death of Lazarus (John 11:31). I, Beverly, moaned, I groaned, and I made weird sounds when my daughter Christine died of cancer. I didn't know you made all those strange grieving sounds.

"Likewise the Spirit helps us in our weakness; for we do not know how to pray as we ought, but that very Spirit intercedes with sighs too deep for words" (Romans 8:26).

In time, and I say take your time, you will calm down and the moaning and groaning will pass, but their presence will always be in your heart. The Lord is beside you, holding your right hand; find comfort in the Lord's presence. "Do not fear, for I am with you, do not be afraid, for I am your God; I will strengthen you, I will help you, I will uphold you with my victorious right hand" (Isaiah 41:10).

Please accept the hugs and love that others offer. It will encourage you. Rely on the Holy Spirit to help you each day to express your grief. If you need to cry, cry! If you need to get angry, throw a pillow. If you feel like bargaining with God and say, "Why me?" He will say, "Because I Am." He is the Almighty but right here when we need Him.

Prayer: O Lord, comfort me. I ask the Holy Spirit to pray for me because I do not know what to pray. Now allow God's presence to come upon you. Take a breath in and say: "Help me, Jesus." Breathe out and say, "Have mercy on me." Repeat. Relax and talk to the Lord, for the Spirit is in you and is waiting for you to ask Him to come in. Say your own prayer, or the Lord's Prayer.

Sing or read "It Is Well with My Soul"
by Horatio G. Spafford, 1873:

"When peace, like a river, attendeth my way,
When sorrows like sea billows roll,
Whatever my lot, thou hast taught me to say
It is well; it is well with my soul.
It is well with my soul;
It is well; it is well with my soul."

THE LORD IS OUR SHEPHERD/ HE CARRIES US

The Lord is my shepherd, I shall not want.
Psalm 23:1

I shall not want. God is with you this day and will provide for you. How has God provided for you physically, mentally, emotionally, and spiritually?

My answer: God has helped me get up, and when *I'm up*, to be God's servant as the Holy Spirit directs me. Mentally and emotionally, I can rest in God's promises that are true. Spiritually, Jesus has redeemed me, made me right in God's sight as I am forgiven, and loved as God's beloved to live forever in His presence.

"God makes me to lie down in green pastures and leads me beside the still waters." (verse 2) Are you tired, restless, anxious, or nervous? God says, "Be still and know that I Am God" (Psalm 46:10). Come rest a while, come be near me, for I created you to love me, to walk with me and trust me. Turn off the music, TV, and phone and just curl up in your resting place and picture the ocean, creek, and waves calming your soul. Give all the unsettled thoughts to God and let them flow and be washed away. Oh, it is so good to experience God's peace: for the Lord *restores my soul.* Pause, reflect, listen, relax, and rest in the Lord's presence.

God, the Father, Son, and Holy Spirit *lead me on the right path.* Do you not see the right path?

"Thus says the Lord: Stand at the crossroads, and look, and ask for the ancient paths, where the good way lies; and walk in it, and find rest for your souls" (Jeremiah 6:16).

Even though I walk through *the darkest valley or through the shadow of death,* I, _____ (your name here), will *fear no evil* for You, Lord, are with me. We walk through. We remember we have survived and our Lord Jesus has helped us walk through the challenges placed before us. I say *us,* for we have been blessed with the help of others (family, friends, church family) to get through these challenges in our life.

I fear no evil: "I have chosen you and not cast you off; do not fear, for I am with you, do not be afraid, for I am your God; I will strengthen you, I will help you, I will uphold you with my victorious right hand" (Isaiah 41: 9a–10). A suggestion: write this Scripture on a memo pad and post where you can see it each day and claim it.

Remember and say to yourself, "Even though I am getting older, and even though life is becoming more difficult as I face daily challenges, I will not fear what lies ahead. I will cast out doubt, thoughts that emerge from nowhere, and pain that tingles in surprising places, for You, Lord, are with me through it all!"

For *your rod and staff: Your rod to* protect and Your staff to guide; they comfort me and carry me. (Amplified)

As you enter my home, on my wall is a picture of Jesus as Shepherd carrying a lamb around His shoulders. It is a beautiful picture showing His love for the rescued lost lamb. Jesus is bringing the lamb home to be with the rest of the flock.

Jesus rescues us, takes us by the hand, and leads us home. Jesus restores us as we are secure in His hand of mercy, grace, forgiveness, and love. Rest in the promises of your Living Savior. Now give Jesus your praise and thankfulness for all He has done for you.

Sing or read the hymn "Savior, like a Shepherd
Lead Us" by Dorothy A. Thrupp, 1836:

Savior, like a Shepherd Lead Us
Much we need thy tender care,
In thy pleasant pastures feed us,
For our use they folds prepare.
Blessed Jesus, blessed Jesus!
Thou has bought us, thine we are.
Blessed Jesus! Thou has brought us, thine we are."

After reciting the hymn, please give your own prayer to your
Shepherd, Jesus, and tell Him how you feel this day. State your
need and give your thankfulness and praise.

Day 23

REST FOR YOUR SOUL
BY SYLVIA BOWER

Come to me, all you who are weary and are
carrying heavy burdens, and I will give you
rest. Take my yoke upon you and learn from
me; for I am gentle and humble in heart,
and you will find rest for your souls. For
my yoke is easy and my burden is light.
Matthew 11:28–30

A yoke is a wooden crosspiece that is fastened over the necks of two animals and attached to a plow or cart that they are to pull. It is impossible for the two animals to pull their load alone. Jesus wants us to realize that we cannot function fully without Him. All through the Bible, God continuously reminds us to *follow Him*! Jesus came to die on the cross that our sins would be forgiven, and we do not have to bear our trials without Him. He remembers sin no more. We are forgiven by the blood of Christ. Whether we realize that when He carries us that there is "Only one set of footprints in the sand," as Mary Fishback Powers poem states. Or that His yoke is easy and His burden is light shows us that we cannot do it alone. I need to surrender myself to Him and rely on Him to do with me whatever He desires. I give up my will, desires, selfishness, pride, and all other self-driven desires for Him to fill me with His wonderful Spirit.

Those sins, thoughts, and burdens that drag you down need to be thrown out and filled with His Word and thoughts and your service to Him. Allow your burden to become light because He is yoked with you! Please remember these mistakes are tossed in the bottom of the sea, never to be brought up again (Micah 7:19).

Prayer: Dear Father, help me relinquish myself to You. Please take my selfishness, pride, greed, and anything that interferes with our relationship and fill me with your Spirit. Let me reach out to serve others as You have taught us to do. Thank you for Your presence in my life and for the rest that You provide for my soul. In Jesus's name, Amen.

Sing or read the hymn
"Near to the Heart of God", Cleland B. McAfee, 1903:

"There is a place of quiet rest, near to the heart of God;
A place where sin cannot molest, near to the heart of God.
O Jesus, blest Redeemer, sent from the heart of God,
Hold us who wait before thee near to the heart of God."

Day 24

ENOUGH! LISTEN

*So do not worry about tomorrow, for
tomorrow will bring worries of its own.
Today's trouble is enough for today.*
Matthew 6:34

*But strive first for the kingdom of God
and His righteousness, and all these
things will be given to you as well.*
Matthew 6:33

Enough already! That's enough! My mind tells me to just keep on
doing one more thing, but my body says, Enough! Stop! Listen,
you don't have to keep pushing. For each day has enough trouble
of its own. Today's agenda is enough for today. Can you relate? So
listen, stop, and praise the Lord for the day's completion.

I like to have a checklist and mark things off as I complete the task. It is a well-done booster marker for me. Yet the Lord tells us to let the Lord be our daily planner. We are to *be still* and let God plan our day. How? First, start your day with the Lord, *listen* to God's instructions, and *follow* the Holy Spirit's directives.

I say, "But I am so quick, so impulsive!"

And the Lord says, "I know you are. Slow down."

Oh, my, how I have slowed down. So I have time to listen if I just take the time. So take a breath and listen before you act, speak, or move, for the Lord will help you in your areas of concern, work, play, conflicts in relationships, and decision making.

But we say, "I want to be in control of all things." Yes, but stop; enough already. You and I are not listening.

So what are the directives? Our directive is for us to listen, and when we listen, we discover that our Lord speaks to us as we listen.

The Lord will speak/counsel you in the night and day as you listen to the Holy Spirit's small still voice:

I will praise the Lord, who counsels me; even at night my heart instructs me. I have set the Lord always before me. Because he is at my right hand, I will not be shaken. Therefore my heart is glad and my tongue rejoices; my body also will rest secure (Psalm 16:7-9 NIV).

You have made known to me the path of life; you will fill me with joy in your presence, with eternal pleasures at your right hand. (Psalm 16:11 NIV).

I have experienced that the Holy Spirit awakens me in the middle of the night. I need to have paper and pencil by my bed so I can record what is being told to me. If I do not record the insight it will be forgotten or remembered incorrectly in the morning. So have your paper and pencil ready as the Lord speaks and directs you.

Prayer: Dear Lord, I can't believe You are so close to me, part of me, intertwined. Help me to remember to stop and listen to You, for I keep forgetting and end up doing my own thing. Help me to pause, to seek your help and wait for your answer and directives. O Holy Spirit, you are so powerful! I need to seek You, believe and be thankful! Help me to stop when the day is done, giving it all to you as I say: "All is well", for You Lord have blessed me. In Jesus's name I pray. Amen.

Say or sing the hymn
"Up from the Grave He Arose, Robert Lowry, 1874:

Up from the grave he arose, with a mighty triumph o'er his foes;
he arose a victor from the dark domain, and he lives forever,
with his saints to reign, He arose! He arose! Hallelujah!
Christ arose!

Day 25

A DEVOTION FROM A CAREGIVER THE FAITH AND FORGIVENESS FORGETFULNESS CAN TEACH BY KATHY MOORE

*Some Pharisees asked Jesus when the Kingdom of
God would come. His answer was, "The Kingdom
of God does not come in such a way as to be seen.
No one will say, 'Look, here it is!' or 'There it is!';
because the Kingdom of God is within you."*
Luke 17:20–22 (Good News Translation)

The pained look on my father's face prompts me to ask, "How are you feeling?" and "Do you have any questions?"

When he responds with, "I don't know" while tapping his forehead, I spare him the probing questions and reply with my usual, this-is-what's-going-on spiel: "Dad, you had a stroke on August 2, 2020. Since then, you have made very few new memories and have difficulty processing and executing your activities of daily living. Diane and I are proceeding with the wishes you outlined in your Living Will. I live with you and I am your medical power of attorney, while Diane is your financial power of attorney. You don't need to pretend that you know what is going on …"

By the time I state the second sentence, I realize I am only saying this to console myself. He cannot process all this, and I like using "med-speak."

The anguish of daily amnesia is heightened when Dad attempts to complete his therapy assignments. Rather than writing down the activity in the moment, Dad reads and rereads all that he has done that day, week, and month and tearfully taps his head: "I am sorry, that's terrible, I can't remember."

I understand the rationale of the therapists' assignments. Repetitive listing along with multiple sensory stimulation may cause memories to "stick." But after nine months, nothing was sticking. My first rebel caregiver decision was to end this assignment. Though I knew he would soon forget this struggle, it was too painful for me to witness this daily, and Dad appears simply blissful when busied in the moment.

As Dad transitions to joyfully reading his devotions and completing tasks as prompted, I observe a "peace beyond understanding." Dad finds a peace in his forgetfulness as if he sees something I don't.

The kingdom of God does not come in such a way as to be seen.

What does my world "look" like (this includes the emotional landscape as well) when I know God is in my midst? As in Jesus's example, it is not free of suffering. When feeling anxiety or pain, I find it is exceedingly difficult to know God is in my midst or within. Frankly, life looks bleak.

Again, my dad is showing me an example of God's kingdom in his amnesia. Amnesia is a blessing when one cannot remember the negative moments. Dad often responds when asked about previously touchy political subjects, "I don't remember what I was so angry about."

I remember this when I have a bad day and become impatient or snippy or, regretfully, a nurse-Ratchet sort. I know he'll forget, and I'll have the opportunity of a do-over. Dad is modeling "forgive and forget." How nice to experience this type of forgiveness. On the other hand, when personal regrets or grudges creep into my head, I practice this type of forgetfulness and can exercise compassion toward myself and others. (I am not suggesting that we forget or erase the past but rewrite the painful story that accompanies it).

No one will say, 'Look, here it is!' or "There it is!'

In desperation, I may spin my wheels seeking, looking here or there (or fill in the blank) for comfort. What does one do or where does one go for comfort or direction when one has no memory of purpose? My dad becomes lost in "what I am supposed to do?" I see him mouth a prayer. A man who was so self-sufficient is now completely dependent on others. Dad must put his faith in my sister and me to carry out his plans. I usually quip with, "You are retired; there is not much you are 'supposed' to do," and redirect him to a gardening task or a puzzle and he smiles. I have another response in which I thank him for trusting me to be his caregiver. I am not as powerful as God either.

As a result, I have been emulating the blind faith my father portrays. It looks like this: I do my daily jobs, speak kindly and skillfully, and forgo the worry. God's in charge, God's in charge … again, this is a liberating and compassionate exercise.

While I am unsure if my dad knows how his stroke amnesia is portraying faith and forgiveness, I believe his love of God gives him peace. I am thankful for the short time I was able to be my father's caregiver and grieve his loss of mental well-being. In closing, and to experience God in our midst, I give you a prayer:

Oh, Blessed Creator, your kingdom is ineffable,

Yet it is here and now.

May I experience the kingdom within.

May I accept the people, places, and events in this moment.

May I experience the peace that passes all understanding.

May the suffering of the world not blind me.

May the suffering of memories not burden me.

May the anxiety for the future not deplete me.

May I embody joy, love, and strength beyond the limits of this physical form.

May I become whole with Your sustenance.

May we experience the kingdom within.

May we accept people, places, and events in this moment …

Thy will be done. I am grateful.

"Do not be anxious about anything, but in everything, by prayer and petition, with thanksgiving, present your requests to God. And the peace of God, which transcends all understanding, will guard your hearts and your minds in Christ Jesus" (Philippians 4:6–7 NIV).

Day 26

INVISIBLE CHRISTMAS GIFTS BY NANCY JOHNSTON

By contrast, the fruit of the Spirit is love,
joy, peace, patience, kindness, generosity,
faithfulness, gentleness, and self-control.
Galatians 5:22–23

Christmas 2020 will be remembered by our family as the Christmas of invisible gifts. COVID-19 kept me house-bound; thus no shopping was done. After pondering what to do, I was moved by the Spirit to give my daughter and each of her family a virtue to be used throughout the year as appropriate. I explained to the grandchildren that their gifts this year would be invisible and are known as virtues. With questionable looks from the younger grandchildren, it was further explained that a virtue is a characteristic—an action you demonstrate, or something you do, feel, or think. Everyone, however, would be given the most important virtue—*love*—as a reminder to *love one another* all year long.

Then each was given a small gift bag with a virtue written on a cutout (from previous Christmas cards). One by one each bag was opened and the virtue revealed. It was read aloud and its meaning discussed. Some of the virtues were patience, hope, kindness, gentleness, and thankfulness. My daughter listed who had what virtue, and everyone agreed to be accountable for their virtue. The last instruction was to keep it with them or put it someplace they would see it periodically as a reminder of their own personal virtue.

It is my hope everyone will be mindful of their virtue and be amazed at how often and in various circumstances they will recall their invisible gift. It's a gift that can be used many times in a positive and meaningful manner as they go about their daily lives.

A game of "Remember Your Virtue" has developed in fun as a family member reminds another of their virtue. And just think—I didn't leave the house to go shopping and didn't spend any money! I am already thinking of other virtues to use next year!

Question: So I ask, which virtue would you pick?

Prayer: Dear Lord, we thank You for family and the many blessings You provide for us. Keep us safe in Your tender loving care, and may we always exalt You by possessing virtues You have given us to lead a life pleasing to You. Amen.

Day 27

LOOKING TO
THE UNSEEN

---

*Now faith is the assurance (the confirmation,
the title-deed) of the things (we) hope for, being
the proof of things (we) do not see and the
conviction of their reality-faith perceiving as
real fact what is not revealed to the senses.*
Hebrews 11:1 (Amplified)

Let's take a positive journey to the unseen. Sit and contemplate what is meant by the unseen and write down your thoughts here.

We read in Scripture that faith is the assurance of things hoped for, the conviction of things not seen. One advantage of being in our senior years is that we have time to contemplate, sit, and be still and invite God's Holy Spirit to speak and embrace the unseen. We believe our faith acknowledges God's promises of the unseen.

"The best and most beautiful things in the world cannot be seen or even touched-they must be felt with the heart!"—Helen Keller.

I see God's constant, unfailing love; Jesus's presence always with us and in us; the Holy Spirit's guidance, conviction, comfort, and assurance; and the inner nudging of the Spirit. Faith is the assurance, knowing with confidence that what is promised will happen. Faith is love, the overflowing love of God in, around, and before us; and is our love flowing out to others through Christ's love in us. Faith unseen is grace, mercy and forgiveness given to us with no price tag, not deserved, but radically given through the sacrificial gift of Christ. It is trust, not relying on our own understanding but on God who will make straight our path.

I am in awe! Are we not all in awe and in grateful thanksgiving and praise to the great I AM (God) who has given us so very much? I am humbled and so grateful to our Loving, Living Father, God, Son, and Holy Spirit. My cup overflows.

We as seniors can look back and see God's hand in our lives and how God has helped us to get through it all. Whether it has been the challenge of divorce, death of loved ones, job and career changes, new locations, changes of church membership, or entry into a retirement community, we discover God has been with us.

Paul tells us to wait patiently in Romans 8: 24: "For in hope we were saved. Now hope that is seen is not hope. For who hopes for what is seen? But if we hope for what we do not see, we wait for it with patience".

Let us again reflect how God has been with us through it all and give God our praise and thankfulness.

Prayer: O Lord, we come giving You the praise for all that You have done for us. You are so present, unseen but alive within us, bringing us hope, forgiveness, grace, mercy, and love. Come and fill us with Your Spirit to help us fix our eyes on You. Help us to vision the unseen. Then direct us to rest in You as we wait for Your return and wait patiently for the unseen to become seen. In Jesus's name we pray. Amen.

Read or sing the psalm "It Is Well with My
Soul" by Horatio G. Spafford, 1873:

"And, Lord, haste the day when my faith shall be sight,
The clouds be rolled back as a scroll; the trump shall
Resound, and the Lord shall descend, even so, it is
Well with my soul. It is well with my soul,
It is well, it is well with my soul."

Day 28

AND THERE IS LIGHT AND LOVE BY REV. JOHN OSBORNE

*Recently, at a spring choral concert, we heard the
anthem "E'en So, Lord Jesus, Quickly Come,"
by Paul O. Manz. The text of this anthem was
arranged by his wife, Ruth, and is based on
Revelation 22.*

Paul and Ruth Manz wrote this anthem in 1953, at a time of great
stress over a family health crisis. It was a time of high anxiety and
personal darkness that tested their faith.

We have all experienced moments of spiritual challenge when
our personal world seems bleak and dark, and we call out to our
Lord for His Presence and light. For well over a year, the whole
world has been in such an experience as we have endured the

Covid-19 pandemic and the resulting upheavals in our personal and societal norms. A time of high anxiety and great stress has tested our faith in many ways. How often we have wondered—aloud, and silently in our prayers—when our Lord would come again to bring us through this experience to a brighter and more hopeful reality, and to a new normal.

We are starting to notice the evidence that our Lord is once again making good on His promise to "come soon." Light is displacing the pervasive darkness, and hope is reaffirmed. Safety guidelines are constantly being adjusted almost daily. We pray we will be returning to something that resembles how things were.

Thanks and praise be to God for the Holy Presence in our lives!

Prayer: Almighty One, who has promised to join us in living this life, continue to help us recognize Your Presence in our daily experience so that our living bears witness to the reality of Your coming soon—again and again. In the name of Christ we pray. Amen.

Day 29

THE LORD'S PRESENCE FOREVER

*Surely or only goodness, mercy and unfailing
love shall follow me all the days of my life; and
through the length of days the house of the Lord
(and His presence) shall be my dwelling place.*
Psalm 23:6 (Amplified)

In his book *A Shepherd Looks at Psalm 23*, W. Phillip Keller says:

> For when all is said and done on the subject of a
> successful Christian walk, it can be summed up in
> one sentence. "Live ever aware of God's presence."
> There is the "inner" consciousness, which can be
> very distinct and very real, of Christ's presence in
> my life, made evident by His gracious Holy Spirit
> within. It is He who speaks to us in distinct and

definite ways about our behavior. For our part it is a case of being sensitive and responsive to that inner voice.----Then there is the wider but equally thrilling awareness of God all around me. I live surrounded by His presence.----- He is conscious of every circumstance I encounter. He attends me with care and concern because I belong to Him. And this will continue through eternity. What an assurance! I shall dwell in the presence of (in the care of) the Lord forever! Bless His name."

When I was a small child, around six years of age, a brilliant, glorious light shined through my window into my room. The Lord's presence surrounded me, and I knew this light was the very presence of the Lord. This God moment impacted my life forever as I passionately desired to serve the Lord. Oh, I never imagined that I would be a woman pastor. I thought back then I would be a missionary or be in BVS (Brethren Volunteer Service). I give God the praise for having been called to serve God as Pastor Bev.

One of the requirements for graduation at United Theological Seminary was to participate in a cross-cultural experience. I chose to go to Russia. Our group stayed and worked at a monastery for several days. My friend and I had the privilege of sweeping the dirt floor in the sanctuary using a whisk broom and brown bag. We gently swept the dirt into the bag so the dust did not rise to the rafters where the ladies were painting the pictures of Bible stories on the walls. Behind us hung a large picture of Jesus facing us.

I ask you to imagine this setting with Jesus facing you. What do you see in Jesus's face?

Jesus says: "I love you; I have forgiven you." (Remember, your sins and shortcomings have been forgiven and are in the bottom of the sea.) "So come and rejoice in my love." Now imagine being in the very presence of Jesus and living with Him forever. Oh, how glorious this will be. Praise the Lord.

God promises you will live forever with Him. Rest in this promise. You don't have to do anything or earn this reward. Jesus has already fulfilled this requirement for you. It is your amazing grace given freely to you through Christ. May you give Jesus your thanks and praise this day.

Prayer: Oh, Lord Jesus, we thank You for all You have done to make it possible for us to live securely and freely with You forever. Help us to keep thanking You and praising Your Holy name. O Lord, we can't imagine facing You as you embrace us, lift us up, and carry us home. Help us not to fear but to rest in Your assurance that Your promises are true. In Jesus's name we pray. Amen.

Sing or say the words to the hymn
"Victory in Jesus" by Eugene M. Bartlett, 1939:

"O victory in Jesus, my Savior forever!
He sought me and bought me with his redeeming blood;
he loved me ere I knew him,
And all my love is due him;
He plunged me to victory beneath the cleansing flood."

Day 30

GOD'S TRIP TICKET

What no eye has seen, nor ear heard, nor
the human heart conceived, what God
has prepared for those who love him.
1 Corinthians 2:9

When I look up and see the radiant clouds with the gorgeous colors and formations, I succumb to God's expression of beauty. I just can't imagine what our loved ones are experiencing in heaven.

Pause, be still, and picture God's promise of a paradise restored.

John 14:3 :Jesus gives us a glimmer of our exciting new venture. Jesus tells us that in His Father's home, there is plenty room for you. "And if I'm on my way to get your room ready, I'll come back and get you so you can live where I live. And you already know the road I'm taking" (The Message).

Jesus promises to take us by the hand and lead us to our new dwelling place to live forever with our God. Jesus tells us that where we will live there will be no more tears, no more pain or death as peace prevails.

In Revelations 21:1–6:

I saw Heaven and earth, new-created, Gone the first heaven, gone the first earth, gone the sea. I saw Holy Jerusalem, new-created, descending resplendent out of Heaven, as ready for God as a bride for her husband. I heard a voice thunder from the Throne: "Look! Look! God has moved into the neighborhood, making his home with men and women! They're his people, he's their God. He'll wipe every tear from their eyes. Death is gone for good—tears gone, crying gone, pain gone—all the first order of things gone." The Enthroned continued, "Look! I'm making everything new. Write it all down—each word dependable and accurate." Then he said, "It's happened. I'm A to Z. I'm the Beginning. I'm the conclusion." (The Message)

My daughters Diane, Kathy, and Christine worked for a travel agency during their summer breaks and mapped out trip tickets for their clients. Oh how fun it was for them to plan exciting trips as the families anticipated their new ventures.

God has already prepared our ticket. God knew us before we were born and knows our destiny. There are no words, for we just can't imagine God's designed future for us. God knows when it is time; so wait patiently, rest, and trust in God's timing, knowing Jesus has paid for the ticket and will escort us home.

Prayer: Oh Lord, I am humbled in anticipation of my next journey with You into the unknown yet known. Help me to trust

You as you have gone before and gotten everything prepared for my journey with You. Remove all fears and doubts and replace them with assurance and peace as I wait and rest in You. In Jesus's name I pray. Amen.

Sing or say the words to
"The Hymn of Promise" by Natalie Sleeth, 1986:

"In the bulb there is a flower,
In the seed, an apple tree; in cocoon, a hidden promise;
Butterflies will soon be free!
In the cold and snow of winter
There's a spring that waits to be, unrevealed until its season,
Something God alone can see.
In our end is our beginning in our time, infinity;
In our doubt there is believing; in our life, eternity.
In our death, a resurrection;
At the last, a victory, unrevealed until its season,
Something God alone can see."

Day 31

PEACE OF GOD

---

*And God's peace (be yours, that tranquil
state of a soul assured of its salvation through
Christ, and so fearing nothing from God
and content with its earthly lot of whatever
sort that is, that peace) which transcends all
understanding, shall garrison and mount guard
over your hearts and minds in Christ Jesus.*
Philippians 4:7 (Amplified)

I ask you to sit still and allow God's Spirit to embrace and enfold
you. Allow God to bring a sense of calmness over your entire
being, body, mind, and soul. Give yourself permission to rest in
silence, and push pause for a while.

Oh, my goodness, as I am sitting still in my recliner, there is
a rainbow illuminating the wall, radiating white streaks on the
cross. I see the colors forming and shaping on the cross. Oh, what

a beautiful sight of God's ever-present reality acknowledging "I am here"!

Peace, I leave with you; My (own) peace I now give and bequeath to you. Not as the world gives do I give to you. Do not let your heart be troubled, neither let it be afraid - stop allowing yourselves to be agitated and disturbed; and do not permit yourselves to be fearful and intimidated and cowardly and unsettled (John 14:27 Amplified).

My peace, oh, the peace that Jesus brings to us is a calmness, an assurance that we know that God's promises are true. Jesus has prepared a place, a new home with our name on it, waiting for our occupancy. As I write this, I am going in July to Wesley Glen Retirement Community, and my name is on the outside door. And my name is on God's dwelling place for me and for you. Praise God! Now relax, rest, and allow God's peace to come and remain on you. Stay as long as you wish.

As we celebrate and remember Easter, we acknowledge Jesus as "I'm up," as He rose from the grave. When He appeared to His disciples, He said to them, "Peace be with you. Why are you frightened, and why do doubts arise in your hearts? Look at my hands and feet; see that it is myself?" (Luke 24:36, 38).

"You too will rise, do not be afraid, for you will be with Jesus, family, and friends where there will be no more tears, death, or crying" (Revelation 21:4).

And Paul tells us in Romans 8:38: "For I am convinced that neither death, nor life, nor angels, nor rulers, nor things present, nor things to come, nor powers, nor height, nor depth nor anything else in all creation will be able to separate us from the love of God in Christ Jesus our Lord."

Prayer: Oh Lord, bring us your peace, the peace that passes all understanding. Help us to rest in Your promises that You will take us home to be with You when it is Your timing. Bring a calmness that engulfs us. Keep us united in You, making all challenges we face possible through You as we continue to live and walk one day at a time. Help us to get *up* and help us walk in the blessed assurance of Your great love. In Jesus's name I pray. Amen.

Sing or read the words to the hymn "Blessed Assurance, Jesus Is Mine!" by Fanny J. Crosby, 1873:

"Blessed assurance, Jesus is mine.
O what a foretaste of glory divine!
Heir of salvation, purchase of God,
Born of His Spirit, washed in His blood.
This is my story, this is my song,
Praising my Savior all the day long;
This is my story, this is my song,
Praising my Savior all the day long."

"The Lord bless you and keep you; the Lord make his face to shine upon you, and be gracious to you; the Lord lift up his countenance upon you, and give you peace" (Numbers 6:24–26).

CONTRIBUTORS

Barbara Davids grew up on a farm in Ohio, graduated from Ohio State in nursing, worked at University Hospital, Columbus, St. Elizabeth Hospital School of Nursing, W. Lafayette, Indiana, Anthem BC-BS, and is retired. She likes to spend time with her two children, three grandchildren, and one great-grandson. She enjoys teaching, reading, music, jigsaw puzzles, traveling, and quiet times at the family tree farm where she grew up.

Rev. Sandra Huber: daughter; sister; wife; mother of two biological, six foster, and one adopted children; grandmother; and friend. Retired deacon, United Methodist Church. BS in education, Eastern Illinois University; graduate studies at Indiana State University, Cleveland State University, Methodist Theological School of Ohio. Taught third grade in Clay County Schools, Brazil, In. and sixth grade in Willoughby-Eastlake schools, Ohio. Served the United Methodist Church of Chagrin Falls in the East Ohio Conference of the United Methodist Church; Troy First and Powell United Methodist churches in the West Ohio Conference of the United Methodist Church.

Eddie Phelps is the surviving spouse of wife, Marva Phelps, and current husband to Susan Phelps. Raised in Lincolnton, NC, he was born into a family of seven. His mother died at an early age, leaving his father and oldest sister to raise them. Eddie is the youngest and only surviving sibling of his brothers and sisters. He is a retiree of General Motors and is a caring dad, husband, and uncle and friend to many.

Rev. Dr. Crystal D. Walker is the only daughter of Eddie and Marva Phelps. She is the mother of three children (one deceased) and two bonus children. She is a member of the clergy and is ordained in the Christian Church (Disciples of Christ). She serves as executive director of Greater Dayton Christian Connections, which is a social justice ministry concentrating on collateral sanctions and anti-racism. She and her husband, Rev. Shelby Walker, are the proud grandparents of ten.

Rev. Beverly Schmidt was born to farming parents in Iowa, married Glen while in college, and moved to Ithaca, New York, after graduation. Glen studied Dairy Science at Cornell and Bev bore five children during that twenty-year period. They moved to Ohio when Glen was promoted to department chair at Ohio State University. A few years later the children were grown and Beverly followed a longstanding call to ministry. She has degrees from the Methodist Theological Seminary in Ohio, Princeton Theological Seminary, and McCormick Theological Seminary in Chicago. She served as pastor in churches in central Ohio and supported college ministry in retirement. Bev also enjoyed a ten-year period working with the Evangelical Church of the

Czech Republic. For the past ten years Bev and Glen have lived in Ohio, at Westminster Thurber Retirement Community. They enjoy their growing family, which includes three beautiful great-grandchildren.

Rev. David Woodyard is a 1957 Westerville High School graduate; 1966 Otterbein College graduate; and 1969 United Theological graduate. Dave pastored UM churches in Bremen (Calvary), Marietta (Norwood), Cincinnati (Northern Hills), and St. Mary's (Wayne St.) and retired in 2003. Dave is now doing congregational care ministry at the Powell UMC. His wife Jean and son Toby are deceased. Dave has a daughter, son-in-law, and two grandsons.

Sue Sheets was raised in Chillicothe, Ohio, and moved to Columbus in 1976. She is a member of Powell United Methodist Church where she assisted in leadership for ladies using Upper Room devotions. She also participated in Villas of Riverbend Women's Bible Study. Sue retired from the State of Ohio Department of Transportation as an office manager.

Sylvia Llewelyn Bower is a registered nurse who practiced nursing in Ohio, Texas, Missouri, Arizona, Tennessee, and Florida. She was certified in case management and nursing administration. She is retiring from Ohio Health. She is an author of three books on celiac disease and is currently on the board of the Gluten Free Gang of Central Ohio, which is a support group for those with celiac disease. Her passions include studying the Bible and serving others, including volunteering at Worthington Christian Village (long-term care) and Kobacher House (inpatient hospice program). She is married to Jack for sixty-four years and has three adult children, six grandchildren, and four great-grandsons.

Kathy Moore is the daughter of Beverly and Paul Avers, mother to Sean and Lindsay. Kathy is a semi-retired registered dietitian nutritionist who has enjoyed working in a variety of settings in Indiana, Michigan, and Ohio. In her free time she loves to experiment in the kitchen, ride her bike in the countryside, and beautify the garden. Kathy wrote this when she was her father's full-time live-in caregiver.

Nancy Johnston with husband, Jim, have one daughter, two grandsons, and three step-granddaughters. Nancy participates in Villas at Riverbend Women's Bible study, a member of Powell United Methodist Church and in Upper Room devotions. She retired from National City Bank.

Rev. John Osborne was born into a parsonage family and began pastoral ministry in 1967. He served parishes in New Winchester, Hamilton (Park Ave.), Westerville (Church of the Master), Prospect, Toledo (Monroe St.), Mason, Huber Heights (Sulphur Grove), District Superintendent of Cincinnati District, Marysville First, and Middletown First. He served on the staff in chaplain's office at Otterbein Retirement Living Community in Lebanon, Ohio. He did a directed study of "Transformational Organizational Change in the Church" through the Center for Parish Development in Chicago. He is certified in gerontological pastoral care by the Center on Aging, Religion, and Spirituality. He married Donna (Frail) Osborn in 1967, and they have two daughters and four grandchildren.

ENDNOTES

———— ❖ ————

A. W. Tozer, *Pursuit of God* (Bloomington: Bethany House Publishers, 2013), 22.

African American spiritual, *I'm So Glad Jesus lifted me,* "The Faith We Sing" (Nashville: Abingdon Press), 2151.

C. Austin Miles, *In the Garden* (Nashville: The United Methodist Publishing House, 1913), 314.

John H. Sammis, *Trust and Obey* (Nashville: The United Methodist Publishing House, 1887), 467.

R. Kelso Carter, *I'm Standing on the Promises* (Nashville: The United Methodist Publishing House, 1886), 374-375.

Joseph M. Scriven, *What a Friend We Have In Jesus* (Nashville: The United Methodist Publishing House, 1855), 526.

Julia H. Johnston, *Grace Greater than our Sin* (Nashville: The United Methodist Publishing House, 1911), 365.

Sarah Young, *Jesus Calling* (Nashville: Thomas Nelson, Inc., 2004), April 1.

Helen Lemmel, *Turn Your Eyes upon Jesus* (Nashville: The United Methodist Publishing House, 1922), 349.

Mark Lowry, *Mary, Did You Know?* (Nashville, J. Countryman, a Division of Thomas Nelson, Inc., 1998).

George W. Cooke, *Down in My Heart* (Sing 'N' Celebrate for Kids, Words and Music, Inc., 1977), 45.

Alfred H. Ackley, *He Lives* (Nashville: The United Methodist Publishing House, 1933), 310-11.

Harry Emerson Fosdick, *God of Grace and God of Glory* (Nashville: The United Methodist Publishing House, 1930), 577.

Sarah Young, *Jesus Lives* (Nashville: Thomas Nelson, 2009), 34.

Audrey Mieir, *His Name is Wonderful* (Nashville: The United Methodist Publishing House, 1959) 174-175.

Sarah Young, *Jesus Calling* (Nashville: Thomas Nelson, 2004), Nov.13.

Beverly Beeghly Avers, *Intertwined: Beverly & Barbara in the Womb* (Lima: Fairway Press, 2014), 25.

Beverly Beeghly Avers, *Intertwined with Jesus* (Lima: Fairway Press, 2019), 49.

Frederick Whitfield, *O How I Love Jesus* (Nashville: The United Methodist Publishing House, 1855), 170.

Anna B. Warner, *Jesus Loves Me* (Nashville: The United Methodist Publishing House, 1860), 191.

Thomas O. Chisholm, *Great Is Thy Faithfulness* (Nashville: The United Methodist Publishing House, 1923), 140.

Clara H. Scott, *Open my Eyes that I Might See* (Nashville: The United Methodist Publishing House, 1895), 454.

Horatio G. Spatford, *It is Well with My Soul* (Nashville: The United Methodist Publishing House, 1873), 377.

Dorothy A. Thrupp, *Savior, Like a Shepherd Lead Us* (Nashville: The United Methodist Publishing House, 1836), 381.

Mary Fishback Powers, *Footprints in the Sand*, October, 1964.

Cleland B. McAfee, *Near to the Heart of God* (Nashville: The United Methodist Publishing House, 1903) 472.

Robert Lowry, "Up from the Grave He Arose (Nashville: The United Methodist Publishing House, 1874) 322-23.

W. Phillip Keller, *A Shepherd Looks at Psalm 23* (Grand Rapids: Zondervan, 2007), 172–73.

Eugene M. Bartlett, *Victory in Jesus* (Nashville: The United Methodist Publishing House 1939), 370.

Natalie Sleeth, *Hymn of Promise* (Nashville: The United Methodist Publishing House 1986) 707.

Fanny J. Crosby, *Blessed Assurance* (Nashville: The United Methodist Publishing House 1873), 369.

Printed in the United States
by Baker & Taylor Publisher Services